The Crazy, Wonderful Things Kids Say

The Crazy, Wonderful Things Kids Say

Tales from the Singing Pediatrician

Arnold L. Tanis, MD
(Doctor Bud)

INDIANA UNIVERSITY PRESS

This book is a publication of

Indiana University Press
Office of Scholarly Publishing
Herman B Wells Library 350
1320 East 10th Street
Bloomington, Indiana 47405 USA

iupress.indiana.edu

The paper used in this publication
meets the minimum requirements of
the American National Standard for
Information Sciences—Permanence
of Paper for Printed Library
Materials, ANSI Z39.48–1992.

Manufactured in the
United States of America

Cataloging information is available
from the Library of Congress

ISBN 978-0-253-03249-2 (paperback)
ISBN 978-0-253-03250-8 (ebook)

1 2 3 4 5   22 21 20 19 18 17

This book is a labor of love. Love for my precious wife,
Maxine, and for my children. But, moreover, the love
for the thousands of children who were my patients.

Were it not for the constant prodding from my wife, or the
expert advice from my editor, Gary Dunham, the book would
still not be finished. I am also grateful for the invaluable help of
my daughter, Elizabeth, and her colleague Brenda Watson.

CONTENTS

PREFACE

Welcome to the thoughts and musings of a practicing pediatrician across a fifty-year career. Arnold L. Tanis, MD, FAAP, affectionately known to all of us as "Dr. Bud," has been recognized by his peers, local and national medical societies, and various civic organizations, along with three generations of appreciative patients and their families.

Dr. Bud, while in active practice as a founding partner in the largest group pediatric practice in the United States, has also been a tireless and successful advocate for children's health care issues. His advocacy focuses on such areas as seat belt safety laws, health education, breastfeeding guidelines and support, immunization practice and requirements, and mental health issues for children and their families.

He has been recognized as a person with medical skills, people skills, and teaching skills—all that is honorable in this dedicated pediatrician and human being.

Edward J. Saltzman, MD, FAAP

The Crazy,
Wonderful
Things Kids Say

Introduction

I guess I was born under a lucky star. My dear mother and father gave me good enough genes to skip two grades in the Chicago public schools, and I was admitted to the University of Chicago after finishing just two years of high school. I was accepted at the medical school of the University of Chicago when I was barely seventeen. In school, then, I seemed the youngest in everything. Nowadays I am the eldest.

I was born in Chicago to Cyril and Ruth Tanis on Ground-hog Day 1929. I was a very happy kid. As an only child, I was the recipient of all the love my parents had to give. Although I had no brothers or sisters, we had a large extended family in the area, and I enjoyed spending time with them. I missed not having a sibling but was very fond of my younger cousins.

My father manufactured various women's accessories, including trimmings and veils for hats and heads. He sold them to department stores like Marshall Fields and always sealed the deals with only a handshake. When making deliveries with him one time, I asked why he never insisted on signed agreements with the department stores. Shaking his head and smiling, my father simply stated that a handshake and trust in others sufficed. And so I grew up respecting the truth. I remember lying to my parents only one time: After receiving a present of high-topped boots with a knife and a little holster, I promptly lost the knife. When my parents asked me where it was, I told them that I just couldn't find it. After being caught, I suffered my one spanking—not for losing the knife, but for not telling the truth. That exclamation point to what my parents had been teaching me has guided me since.

From my earliest years, I have always burned with curiosity and loved to learn. When I was about eleven years old, one day I decided on the spot to visit the Oriental Institute of the University of Chicago. Determined, I took the bus alone all the way to the south side of the city. My parents were waiting at the museum. I learned later that they had followed me in their car to see what I was up to. We spent the rest of the day together, the first of many wonderful outings to museums.

I loved growing up in Chicago. Let's face it, the Cubs will always be the team for whom I root! Did you know that I was at Wrigley Field with my dad during the World Series in 1945? Because the pitcher disregarded *my* screams to walk Hank Greenberg, famous slugger of the Detroit Tigers, Greenberg responded by hitting a home run. I remember yelling, frustrated, from the sidelines, "We lost the game and series and went down in *ignominy*!" Seventy-one years later, my Chicago Cubs thrilled me with a World Series victory.

I went to the University of Chicago for a special program they sponsored for high school students. When I graduated from high school, I also had a college degree. Shortly afterward,

the Medical School of the University of Chicago accepted me as a student.

Why did I choose medicine as a career? Looking back, it seems I was always following that path. At the age of seven or eight, someone left medical pamphlets and charts of the innards of the body on our back porch. I read every pamphlet and was fascinated by the pictures, especially of the intestines. Another exposure to medicine came from my dear uncle Harry, who owned a drugstore with his two brothers. Besides drinking black cows (floats made with root beer and vanilla ice cream) from the soda fountain, I enormously enjoyed slipping behind the counter to watch Uncle Harry compound pharmaceuticals. One bright summer afternoon, he held up in front of me a pill with a hair in it. Explaining that this pill had been made in someone's basement in Chicago, he told me firmly that one would not find such abnormalities in the work of the pharmaceutical companies. Later, at the age of twelve, I learned firsthand more about the value of a medical career from a visiting nurse. I had been quarantined at home for several weeks after coming down with chicken pox at Boy Scout camp. The example of that kind and able nurse, along with our numerous conversations about medicine and her work, pushed me further down the path to a medical career.

I was and will always be very grateful to the great medical school at the University of Chicago, which gave me the perfect start in practice. It was an outstanding institution, where respect hung heavily in the halls. I began as a very conscientious but average student, coming home during the weekends and playing pinochle or hearts with my parents. While other parents were pressuring their children to study, mine encouraged me to play cards!

My grades improved significantly in the last two years of medical school after entering the clinics, where I came into contact with actual patients; that interaction continued into my rotating internship. (Nowadays medical students have real-life patients from their first year—it makes a difference.) Seeing them opened up a whole new vista to me. Now I was part of the action, though I felt the presence of my professors looking over my shoulders with every patient I saw. I especially liked the kids, because they acted normal and natural and didn't have an agenda. They were themselves. Before I knew it, I had decided to become a pediatrician.

In my fourth year of medical school, I worked in the all-night emergency room at Inland Steel in East Chicago. There, not surprisingly, I gained experience in suturing lacerations and keeping my composure in emergencies. I worked there the equivalent of one week every month.

I wanted to do my internship at a private hospital and my residency at a teaching hospital, where I assumed the education would be better—or at least different. I interned at Michael Reese Hospital in Chicago and completed my residency at Northwestern Children's Memorial Hospital. It was at that time when Dr. Louis W. Sauer, famous for perfecting the vaccine to prevent whooping cough, showed me how to give a shot.

And then my country called. During the Korean War, I was drafted to go into service while a senior in medical school. The dean of the school wrote the government asking them to allow me to finish school. During my internship, the head of Michael

Reese Hospital requested the same temporary deferment. The third time I heard from the draft board, I was in my pediatric residency, so the medical chief of staff made yet another deferment request. Ultimately, we were able to defer the actual draft date until I could be of more service to my country as a fully trained medical doctor. Once my residency was completed and I had started practicing as a pediatrician in Chicago, I received a fourth letter from the draft board. Now married to my beautiful Maxine, but feeling an obligation to serve, I joined the navy.

One of the first steps for new recruits when joining the navy was to list their preferences for where to be stationed. I chose Chicago, Key West, and San Diego, in that order. I thought Chicago would be best because I could still practice pediatrics at my office on the weekends. I selected San Diego and Key West because of the climate; as a bonus, my uncle George and aunt Fanny lived in South Florida.

Boy, I changed my mind quickly. The next time I reported to the Great Lakes Naval Base, the area was experiencing a "Chicago winter." Brrrr—very, very cold and plenty of snow. It was excruciatingly difficult trying to start my car and get it out of its parking spot, so I ended up taking a streetcar to the elevated train, where I got off at the station nearest the base. After resolutely traversing frozen tundra larger than a football field to get to the base, I marched right up to the Wave who had taken my application the previous day and asked if I could change my location preferences. Giving another Wave a knowing look, she shrugged and made the change. As a result, I spent two pleasant years serving my obligation in the great United States Navy stationed in Key West, Florida.

Upon reporting to the executive officer at the Key West Naval Base, I was informed that I would be doing pediatrics during the day but every fifth night would have the "OB watch." I shook my head, puzzled. Did he mean OD watch, the "officer of the day"? I quickly learned that OB watch meant I would be delivering babies.

I stared at the executive officer. "Sir, I have never delivered a baby," I admitted.

He looked at me for a moment. "You will," he replied curtly, turning back to his paperwork.

Over the next two years, I delivered 172 babies.

Having a naval air base at Key West (on Boca Chica Key) meant that everyone had relatively free access to travel. Once, when coming back from a medical convention in Chicago, I got stranded 150 miles from home at the marine air base in Opa-Locka, near Hialeah, Florida. I had called my wife, Maxine, and asked her if she would arrange for a naval pilot from Key West to pick me up. All alone at an enormous airfield on a Sunday afternoon, after an interminable wait and growing panic, I finally spotted a plane coming from the direction of home. It landed, the cabin door flung open, but the plane kept moving. I dashed after the plane, threw my Val-pak into the cabin, and jumped onboard. I barely got the door closed when the plane was back in the air. I tried to make small talk with the pilot, but he frowned and ignored me. After landing, I tried to thank him, but he remained silent.

I later learned from Maxine the reason for his surliness. She had called a number of pilots, all of whom were busy. Now desperate, she reached a pilot's wife who, she discovered, knew me. A few weeks earlier, the wife of a lieutenant commander had come into my pediatric office in tears. Her fifteen-year-old son had been admitted to the hospital with chicken pox. She was not allowed to visit him, because it was a contagious disease. After I calmed her down, we walked over to the hospital, arm in arm. I managed to get her into the room to see her boy. After speaking to my wife, this same dear lady had promptly removed the steak she was serving her husband and announced that he could finish it after he brought me back to Key West.

After leaving the service in January 1957, I began private practice as a pediatrician in Hollywood, Florida. I sought out a partner who could tend to the business aspects of the profession. Edward J. Saltzman, MD, FAAP, who would go on to win national awards in the office management of pediatrics, was the ideal choice. Once we met, we knew we would work well together and the practice would thrive. For all of those years we were actively in practice, Eddie and I trusted and had confidence in each other, fitting together like hand in glove. What a wonderful relationship. He is the brother I never had.

Because of our success practicing together, over the next ten years we added a third pediatrician, Robert Pittell, to the office, then a fourth and fifth, and eventually even more. We soon relocated our pediatric practice to a larger office, began adding new locations, and opened the office on weekends. Pediatric Associates, which "growed like Topsy," now boasts more than 35 pediatric medical offices and some 250 doctors throughout Florida.

The greatest reward for me, of course, has been the children—three generations of them. Nearly every day of my fifty-four years of practice, the girls and boys I saw and treated inevitably said or did things that were amusing and charming. We know that there's nothing more original and unfiltered than what children say—they just belt it out.

Take, for example, a five-year-old gentleman perched on his hospital bed, dressed in a cowboy suit and packing two toy guns. At the time, I was a senior medical student on the pediatric floor at the University of Chicago Medical School; down the hall was the medical research laboratory. Suddenly the boy grabbed his guns, pointed them down at the floor, and solemnly announced, "Don't worry, Doctor, I'll get him." A mouse escapee from the laboratory scampered by us, oblivious to being in the crosshairs of a determined sharpshooter.

Another time, as a resident, I was examining an eleven-year-old young man who had an ear complaint. Hmmm . . . the earwax sure looked funny in color, so I carefully removed it.

Oh, my goodness. I held up the object that was causing his pain—a pencil eraser!—in front of the young man. Very calmly, I asked, "When did you put this in your ear?"

"Well . . . ," the boy said, scrunching up his face in thought. "In second grade," he concluded with an innocent smile.

Yes, I just had to know. "What grade are you in now?"

"Fifth."

I looked over at his mother. She stared at her son, face pale, her mouth struggling to say something.

You see what I mean? Soon, I began writing down these wonderful stories, gathering them up in the same way that I seem to have collected lots of other things—leaves, stamps, coins, and whatnot. And I started sharing them. Two years into my practice, I was at home one night having supper with the family. My wife asked our kids to tell me what happened at school that day. After they eagerly poured their hearts out, I smiled and replied, "That's nothing compared to what happened in the office today!" I told them a funny story of what a child patient had said to me that morning, and everyone roared with laughter. Thus arose the beginning of a nightly family tradition, where I would tell stories of particularly funny and memorable things I had heard from my little patients. Whatever my kids encountered during the day, it seemed I always had a better story from the office! Eventually my family began clamoring for the stories to be compiled in a book.

So here you have it. If you enjoy these tales from five decades of treating and listening to children, thank my kids and my most resolute, amazing wife.

When people ask me why I chose pediatrics, I have but one answer. I didn't choose pediatrics; it chose me. I was born to be a pediatrician.

Tales from the
Examining Room

The Singing Doctor

Every doctor has certain peculiarities with which he is associated. I liked to sing in the office, particularly my suture song, which I bellowed out while stitching up a patient.

A fourteen-year-old boy whom I had stitched up three years earlier reappeared in the emergency room. I thoroughly scrubbed my hands and approached the young man. Standing up, he looked directly at me, arms folded, and proclaimed, "Stitching, yes; singing, *no!*"

Such a hurtful statement. "Ahem," I sniffed, "I sing for myself and not for you." I then began to yodel out, "There was blood on the saddle, and blood all around, and a great big puddle of blood on the ground."

He covered his ears as I sang and stitched him once again.

* * *

Six-year-old Oliver pleaded, "Please don't sing."
"I don't sing for you, but for myself," I replied.
"But I said please," he begged.

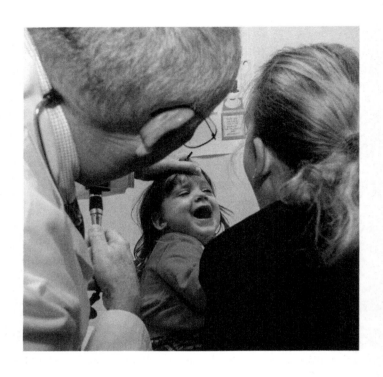

Those Awful, Nasty Shots

Children almost universally abhor immunization injections. For that matter, any kind of shot is looked upon with utter disgust and often terrifying fear by the intended recipient. What can a pediatrician do? Just get it done.

"What hurts you?" I asked five-year-old Joseph, a very bright and articulate lad. I want children themselves to tell me what is wrong with them.

Looking suspiciously at me, the young boy replied, "Shots."

*   *   *

After her physical examination, five-year-old Stephanie announced, "I don't want a shot; it'll hurt."

"No, it really won't," I said confidently.

She was having none of it. "Yes, it will. It'll hurt. I will have a little hole."

*   *   *

"I hate boosters," twelve-year-old Richard declared. "It's the principle of the thing."

*   *   *

Walking out of the examining room, Jessica, eleven years of age, looked up at her mother. "I got so many shots," she whispered, "we can play dot to dot."

* * *

"After your shots today," I reassured Tareah, eleven years old, "you won't get another one for a long time."

She folded her arms and stared at me. "Until I am forty-five."

* * *

The brother of thirteen-year-old Timothy taunted him that he had to get a "booboo" (meaning a shot).

Timothy looked at me and shrugged. "I laugh in the face of a booboo."

* * *

"We need hemoglobin from you, Tori," I said to the nearly nine-year-old.

She shook her head vigorously. "I'd rather walk on glass, barefooted, so you can get my blood."

* * *

I offered six-year-old Joshua a profound choice: "We can give you the booster shot between your eyes or in your arm."

"My brain's starting to hurt," he groaned.

* * *

Nine-year-old Chrystal was being teased by her older sister in the examining room. The girls' mother tried to put a stop to it. "Leave Chrystal alone or I'll have Doctor Tanis give you a shot," she warned.

Her oldest daughter rolled her eyes. "Only if it makes me smarter."

*   *   *

Mrs. R. and her seven-year-old son, Angelo, were seeing me one bright summer morning. "When is he due for his shots?" the mother asked.

"Eleven," I replied casually, making a few more notes.

Angelo suddenly stopped in his tracks and looked up frantically at the clock. "At eleven o'clock?" he gasped.

Well, I guess I should have been more explicit in differentiating between years and hours.

*   *   *

Deana, a young lady who in three days would celebrate her fifteenth birthday, was in the office complaining of a stomachache. During the course of the examination, I discovered she had inflamed ears. She had been seen two weeks previously for a stomachache and headache. Because of the persistence of the stomachache, I decided to measure her sed (sedimentation) rate.

"Well, please don't ruin this finger, because it still hurts from last time," she complained, holding up the aggrieved digit.

"Well, I wasn't really thinking of the finger . . . ," I began slowly, looking at her arm.

"No, no, no!" She begged and pleaded until I changed the subject and spoke of the medicine for her ears.

"I hope you have forgotten about the blood," she said, hopefully, a few minutes later.

I smiled. "We old elephants never forget."

"So be a young one and forget," she retorted.

*   *   *

Six-year-old Mindy came into the office because of an allergic reaction. Her face was swollen and had a fine little papular (elevated) rash similar to prickly heat. Mindy's a good sport but really objects to getting injections. Whenever I see her, she'll ask a dozen times, "Do I have to get a shot, do I have to get a shot, do I have to get a shot?"

This time while I was examining her, she simply looked at me and proclaimed, "My face is not ready for a shot."

*   *   *

I walked into an examining room for an after-hours visit to see little Shana, four years old, whom I had never treated before. She stared at me, sized me up, and announced, "I don't want a shot."

Leaning out the door, I shouted down the hallway to no one in particular, "She doesn't want a shot!"

Stepping back into the room, I asked, "Is there anything else?"

"Yes," she nodded gravely. "My mommy wants me to go to McDonald's."

* * *

Maria, the sixteen-year-old daughter of a longtime established family in my practice, came in to see me. She had a multitude of complaints: coughing, back and chest pain, and some rectal bleeding a couple of days ago.

After examining her thoroughly, I told her and her mother, "We want to get a chest x-ray to be sure that the pain and the cough isn't anything of a serious consequence. I also want to get a blood count, too, to see if the abdominal pain is of serious origin." The latter meant, of course, taking blood from her arm.

Maria began screaming at her mother, "No, I am not going to have it done! I am not going to have it done!"

"Well, it is important," the mother said soothingly. "You have to have it done, and you *will* have it done."

"No, I am sixteen, and I don't have to have anything I don't want!" wailed her daughter, now trying to get up and leave.

"You have to have it!" the mother exclaimed.

"I am a hemophiliac," Maria whimpered, settling back down. "You can't do it."

That went nowhere with us. She then made one last, valiant effort.

"Mom, if you love me you won't do it."

Hugging her, her mother murmured, "We are doing it *because* I love you."

* * *

I examined Shana, a four-year-old young lady, for an upper respiratory tract infection. After I finished, she glared at me, wagged a finger under my nose, and declared, "No pushing needles in!"

* * *

Marc, Todd, and Joshua were in for their complete preschool checkups. It was always quite the annual event, and, as usual, the boy's mother and I had a great time catching up. Mrs. F. confided that Todd's main health concern was an allergy in the morning.

The ten-year-old boy quickly interrupted us. "No, my main concern is getting a shot."

* * *

Jason, a clever fourteen-year-old, was due for a booster as part of his physical examination. He kept staring at the syringe and couldn't stop talking about it as I examined him.

"Are you sure I have to get a shot?"

"Why don't I just come back for it."

"Maybe next year will be a better year."

When we finished the complete physical examination, he walked over and picked up the syringe.

"Don't touch that!" his father admonished him.

"Yes, it's frightfully expensive," I admitted.

Putting it down, Jason looked at us and asked, "Well, then, are you sure you want to waste it on me?"

* * *

Laurie had received a tetanus booster four years ago. Her mother told me that it had taken three people to hold her down.

"Don't be disappointed," I said to the worried daughter. "You don't need a booster now, but you will need it next year."

"It will take more to hold me down," little Laurie promised.

* * *

As they walked into the examining room, Mrs. V. smiled and assured her five-year-old son, Austin, "You don't have to get any shots today."

"Thank you," her little boy solemnly replied. "Shots are my enemies."

* * *

After Robert, at the age of just under five, received his DPT (diphtheria, pertussis, tetanus) booster, he complained, "My bone hurts."

As his mother and I tried to reassure him, he interrupted us. "It would be much better with a Slurpee," he said slyly.

The Little Wise Ones

Never underestimate the mental function of your patients, even the quite young ones. Some kids have fantastic imaginations. The wisdom of my little patients never fails to amaze me.

Pointing to his head, nine-year-old Steven explained an important fact to me and his mother: "I can only tell that the brain is there; not if it is being used. It is in geography."

*   *   *

Six-year-old Alexandra, a second-generation patient, confided to her mother that she loved swimming in the ocean: "Mommy, I think it's part of my spirit."

*   *   *

Mrs. L. revealed to me the great difference in her children's appetites. Jacqueline was a finicky eater, while five-year-old Alex had a great appetite.

Turning to Alex, I just had to ask. "Is your tummy full?"

"Yeah," he promptly replied, "but I am still hungry in my mouth."

*   *   *

While I was chatting with his mother, four-year-old Garrett overheard that she had changed her name when she married. He thought about it for a bit.

"Mommy," the little boy eventually asked quietly, tugging at her hand, "what was my name when I was a baby?"

*   *   *

I was examining Marrinsa, who was three years old. The little lady said she wanted to tell me a secret. I leaned in to listen.

"My nose doesn't work when my eyes are closed," she whispered.

*   *   *

I asked six-year-old Dillon, "Does anyone in your house smoke?"

He thought for a moment, and then, in one big breath, out flew everything on his mind. "My mom and dad, but my dog doesn't. Can I ask you something? How much do you get paid?"

*   *   *

One day, in the middle of a routine checkup, seventeen-year-old Jake suddenly sat up and gave me an intense look. "Your life is a piece of art, Doctor," he said, in a serious, low tone. "What you make of the canvas is your doing."

I stared back at him for a long, silent moment. Nodding, he lay back down and we continued.

*   *   *

I asked five-year-old Emily, "Do you swim?"

"Yes!" she replied enthusiastically, "and I drink water!"

* * *

"When is your birthday?" I asked Richard, a fine young gentleman who was seven years old.

"Every year," he responded quickly, baffled why anyone would ask so obvious a question.

* * *

Five-year-old Jeremiah had come in to see me for a recheck on a laceration of his lip, which had occurred two days ago and had been sewn up by a physician in the emergency room. At the time I saw him, there was redness and some induration, which is a firmness reflecting a secondary infection. Even though I shun the use of antibiotics, there was no alternative this time. Jeremiah became very upset when I told him that because of the infection, he couldn't go to visit his grandmother.

He had calmed down by the time he returned to the office the next day. The little boy proudly announced that he was much better, and indeed he was. I examined his lip; although the swelling persisted, the redness and induration had disappeared.

With a truly inspired, dramatic flourish, I held up my hands and proclaimed, "Oh, my, it is the magic of my hands! I touched you yesterday and now you are so much better!"

Pausing respectfully for a moment, he looked up at me and shook his head sorrowfully. "No, it's the medicine."

* * *

Genevieve, a four-year-old, sat in the room as I examined her young brother, Carlos. "Doctor Tanis," she asked, tugging at my lab coat, "can I have some water?"

"Let me finish examining your brother first," I replied, not looking at her, "then we will get you some water."

The second I concluded the examination, little Genevieve jumped up and stood in front of me, hands on hips. "Now," she said firmly, "let's talk with water."

* * *

And then there was the time I insulted a doll, not once, but twice.

When I had examined little Robin, she clutched her Cabbage Patch doll. I remember making a little teasing remark about it being the ugliest-looking thing I had ever seen—which it indeed was. When she returned a few days later, her mother took me aside and said that her child had been in tears in the car because I had insulted her baby. So, after apologizing to Robin, this time I examined the doll along with her.

Five months later, she returned with an ear infection, still carrying that ugly Cabbage Patch doll. She insisted during the examination that I weigh the doll. I adjusted the scale and did just that—1 pound, 1½ ounces.

Handing the doll back to her, I frowned and complained, "What am I doing this for? I went to medical school, I had an internship, I took a residency, and I'm the former chief of staff of the hospital."

She paused for a moment and gave me an unreadable look. "I beg your pardon?" she finally inquired, drawing her baby close.

* * *

Young Miss Robin, age seven, came to see me because she had a fever. Her fever was not as important to her as was the fact that it might get in the way of her evening plans with two friends—going out for dinner and then sleeping over. More excitement awaited her the next day, when she was to help host an ice-skating party for twenty young friends and their parents.

I examined her. Her throat was red, but the quick ten-minute strep culture test fortunately was negative. I concluded that she most likely had a virus that would take care of itself.

What to do about her big plans? I have preached for decades not to expose healthy children to someone who has an infection. I would not have sent her to school, but there are sometimes mitigating circumstances when one has to yield and bend.

In order to have Miss Robin comprehend my feelings, I asked her if she liked her two girlfriends.

"Oh, yes," she replied, "very much, because I've known them all year long at school."

Well, then, did she want to give them a fever and an infection?

Her response was immediate: "Oh, absolutely not!"

Having made my point, I cautioned her to be careful making physical contact with them and to turn her head the other way when coughing or near them.

Nodding thoughtfully, the seven-year-old paused and looked at me. "This is a test," she began, speaking slowly and softly. "In case I don't do it right, I know I'll never be able to entertain my friends again."

Her profound statement surprised me; even more so as she continued speaking. "My dream came true. I asked God, and I begged God to allow me to have my friends over and my party. He heard me, he listened."

And with that, she left, head held high.

* * *

I was about to enter an examining room to see a patient when I overheard a little girl chatting in another room. She asked, "Why did the cat cross the street?"

I popped my head in the door. "To get to the other side," I blurted out.

Jumping up, she put her hands on her hips and glared. "I didn't say a chicken!" she retorted.

* * *

While in the waiting room, David, age five and a half years, spied a little child and offered an insight born of rich experience: "You're wearing one of those saggy diapers that leak."

* * *

An older patient, Paul, now twenty-three, came in with a laceration in his foot and possibly glass in it. Gently searching for the glass, I decided to philosophize a bit to the young man.

"Life isn't easy, Paul."

My patient sighed. "It's easy, Doctor," he muttered, "just not cheap."

*   *   *

I had seen Jennifer, five years of age, because of a fever, sore throat, and a recheck of an ear infection. When she returned after her medication ran out, she and her younger sister asked very alert and pertinent questions, which I tried to field with intelligent answers. Impressed with both of them, I looked at their mother and began, "These girls are . . ."

At which point Jennifer chirped up: "Terrific?"

*   *   *

I walked into the examining room to see little Thomas, a boy of two and a half years. He immediately jumped up and announced, "Mom, I'm going to the bathroom; you sit and talk to Doctor Tanis."

*   *   *

Six-year-old Heather and her father were waiting for me in the examining room. Spying a urine sample on the table, I picked it up as if to drink it and asked, as I usually do, "Heather, is this orange juice?" When she giggled, her father chortled, "Well, it used to be."

After we all had a good laugh, I followed up with another question to my young patient. "Heather, are you married?"

"No."

"Are you engaged?"

"No." Opening her mouth, she pointed to her six-year-old dentition with a prominent missing tooth. "I'm just a kid."

*   *   *

I had finished with a complete examination on seven-year-old Craig. While I was writing up his chart and filling out the school forms, he accidentally belched.

Before his mother had a chance to say anything, Craig shrugged. "Boys are boys, Mom," he explained.

*   *   *

Nine-year-old Daniel had returned after bilateral acute otitis media, an ear infection. Both ears had been infected, so I was looking at his tympanograms. These are graphic tracings to demonstrate whether or not there is fluid behind the eardrum.

Very pleased with the results, I exclaimed, "Whooooo!"

Daniel looked up at his mother. "Boy," he whispered to her, "I thought he was looking at a *Playboy*!"

*   *   *

Four-year-old Lynn was in the office because of extreme congestion and coughing. I prescribed an anti-mucous medicine and my favorite chest loosener, Organidin drops. I usually recommend so many drops in a Coke or juice every three hours.

"Let's put five drops in a Coke . . . ," I began.

"Not in Coke!" Lynn interrupted, loudly. "Coke sucks!"

I looked at her in utter disbelief. Most of my little patients throughout the years love Coke as the vehicle for taking their medicine.

The mother leaned down toward her daughter. "Lynn, honey, tell Doctor Tanis where Daddy works."

Looking up at me, the little girl proudly said, "For Pepsi Cola."

*   *   *

I liked to ask children what their parents do for a living. Six-year-old Alexandra's answer was precious: "Daddy sends the people to heaven; mommy stays and helps the ones who are crying."

Her father worked in a funeral home.

*   *   *

Mrs. McA. and her eight-year-old daughter, Juliana, were having a discussion with me in the office. The girl could not stay still and was touching and moving everything around her.

"You're turning everything upside down," the mother complained.

Juliana stopped and looked intently at her. "It's my job, Mom."

*   *   *

I had asked nine-year-old Justin if he snored.

"Not me," he replied, a bit defensively, "but Grandma snores loud enough to suck all the paint off the walls."

*   *   *

Eugene was complaining of chest pain, so I sent him to the laboratory for a chest x-ray and CBC (complete blood count) test.

"You should take your shoes with you," I called after him as he scampered away.

Without breaking stride, my ten-year-old patient continued down the hall and tossed back, "That's what mothers are for."

* * *

I asked a new patient, Daniel, to please take his chart down to the lab. Glancing at it, the young man looked puzzled.

"This chart has my brother's name on it," he said.

"Is it Guido?" I confirmed. He nodded.

"Is your father's name Guido?"

Looking down at the chart, Daniel answered, "Yes, and so is my grandfather's. It seems to run in the family."

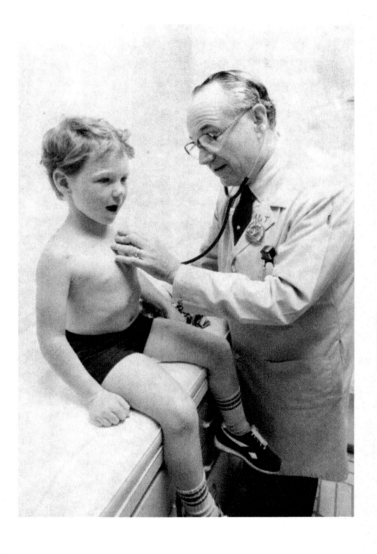

Little Patients with Little Patience

I paid close attention to patients when they told me about their complaints. A lesson I learned early on: listen to the children; they will tell you what's wrong. Well, most of the time. Sometimes they performed dizzying verbal gymnastics to try to wiggle out of treatment.

Philip interrupted his mother, who was relating his medical history to me. "Let me tell the story! It's *my* story, and it's *my* hives!"

* * *

I opened the conversation with nine-year-old Amanda by asking her to tell me what was wrong: "Do we have any complaints?"

She shrugged, looked at her mother, and replied, "I want a pony."

* * *

After a physical examination for vomiting and fever, I asked Anthony, four years of age, "Where does your tummy hurt?"

"All over," he grumbled, wagging a finger at me. "Don't ever do it again."

*   *   *

Katherine, almost four years old, was spinning my round examining chair before I came into the room. As I entered, I heard her mother exclaim, "Katie, I don't want to see you spinning that!"

"You don't have to look," Katie answered sharply.

*   *   *

Teenagers are not always the most cooperative. Greg, fourteen years of age, came into the office once with conjunctival irritation. "Will you put drops in your eyes two times a day?" I asked him.

Shrugging, Greg said, "Depends upon which day."

*   *   *

Eight-year-old Michelle had an urticarial rash (hives), which can be very itchy. When I walked into the examining room, Michelle looked up at me and confessed, "I feel like a tomato with bumps."

*   *   *

Clarence, four-and-a-half years old, had been discharged from the hospital for reactive airway disease, sinusitis, and an ear infection. I first examined him sitting, and then I gently laid him down to check his ears. Lying there, he stared at the ceiling and muttered, "I am getting too big for this."

*   *   *

On a Saturday morning, ten-year-old Erin came into the office for a return appointment. "My day is ruined!" she exclaimed as I walked into the examining room.

*   *   *

Five-year-old Shane pointed to his skin rash. "The ants are making me have chicken pox," he grumbled.

*   *   *

Gabrielle, age three, is always nice to the nurses. She announced to her mother, however, that she would be "mean to the doctor" so that she could go home.

*   *   *

I asked four-year-old Emily how she liked her medicine, the Triaminic purple, a grape-flavored cough syrup.

"Purple makes me sour," she complained. "Purple makes me angry."

*   *   *

Finished examining eight-year-old Shelby, I remarked, "I'd like you to come back in one month."

Shelby immediately shook his head. "I think I am booked," he said hastily.

*   *   *

Having completed my examination of John, age three, I began making notes and speaking to his mother. "Wait," he pleaded, looking up and waving at me. "I am not done yet."

* * *

Five-year-old Shira announced loudly as I entered the examining room, "No x-rays, no shots, no hand blood!"

Her mother prodded gently, "Shira, tell him why."

"I have my freedom!" Shira declared, frowning at me.

* * *

After examining his nose and throat, I instructed five-year-old Justin to lie down so I could check his ears and abdomen.

As my young patient stretched out, he uttered, "Aahhhhh, this is the life."

* * *

The mother of eleven-year-old Zachary confirmed that he needed his hearing checked. I said to Zachary, "Put your feet together and bend over and touch your knees."

Zachary complied. "Well, that must have been the hearing test," he smirked.

* * *

Stuart, fifteen years old, was waiting for me in the examining room. "Stuart, why are you here, sir?" I asked, cheerfully.

He looked down at his feet. "Just 'cause I felt like coming," he mumbled.

* * *

A four-year-old boy had torticollis (a twisted neck) secondary to cervical lymphadenopathy (a condition of the lymph nodes); therefore, I needed to get a throat culture and a CBC (complete blood count). The little one didn't say a word as I poked and prodded.

As I began writing up my notes, the child asked, "Are we going to go home now?"

"Yes," I replied.

"Thank God," the boy replied, resolutely turning his back on me and stalking away.

* * *

I took my time chatting with April, ten years of age, reviewing a whole series of healthy habits. Suddenly, she grabbed my arm.

"You're killing me here," she hissed.

* * *

I instructed thirteen-year-old Melissa, "Jump up on the examining table, if you please, if you please."

Melissa shook her head. "I don't please," she countered, hands firmly on hips.

* * *

Edison, nearly four years old, was in the office because of pneumonia. His grandmother had heated some soup and offered it to him. The coughing, stuffed-up little boy shook his head vigorously. "I don't want no soup," he announced to her.

Edison then turned to me. "And I don't have no blood pressure."

* * *

Rueben, four years old, complained of a headache. He asked me for a Band-Aid to put on his brain.

* * *

Eleven-year-old Aaron came into the office because he was vomiting. "Does your tummy hurt anywhere?" I asked.

Aaron pointed to his navel. "Only here, where the 'intesticles' are," he explained.

* * *

I examined little Alexis, a five-year-old patient who had returned to have his ears and throat rechecked. He was eating a chocolate sandwich cookie when I walked into the examining room.

"Alexis," I began, "you are going to hide the true condition of your throat from me, because it will all be covered with chocolate and I won't be able to tell." He kept eating.

I finished examining him and reviewing his chart. He looked so well that I said, "Well, I think that you can go home now and that I don't have to recheck your blood. I'm sure it is okay."

Looking up at me, he reached for another cookie. "I have chocolate in my blood," he concluded.

*   *   *

I had finished examining Eleanor, who was almost four years of age and had an ear infection. In addition to the antibiotic, I prescribed Auralgan, a medication used to relieve the local pain. I cheerfully informed the mother, "This medicine is good until she gets married."

No sooner were the words out of my mouth than I heard a response: "Mommy, I don't want to get married."

*   *   *

When we draw a blood culture, the skin site is prepared and sterilized with medication. Similarly, when we do a urine culture, we have the patient wash carefully either the vaginal area of a little girl or the tip of the penis of a little boy.

I had told a dear patient, Jon, ten years old, that we needed a stool culture. I was pleased that he could provide a sample right away, as the urge to go seems to disappear in the doctor's office.

As he turned to go, Jon stopped and looked back at me. With a twinkle in his eye, he asked innocently, "Do I have to wash my butt first?"

*   *   *

When I entered examining room #1, four-year-old Ben immediately turned to his mother and said, "Hope I won't be embarrassed."

What did he mean? Shrugging her shoulders, the mother could only repeat to me what her son had said. As she was talking, he turned beet red with, yes, embarrassment. To this day, I don't know why.

* * *

A pediatrician never really knows what he will encounter during the course of an office visit. I went into the examining room to recheck seven-year-old Maximina, who had had strep throat. As I was going to finish a complete examination on her during the recheck, I decided that it would be best to take off the top straps of her little one-piece sun suit. When I did, I looked down and discovered that she apparently had no navel. A nickel, a five-cent piece, covered it.

* * *

I was examining Lee, a sixteen-year-old young man from one of my favorite families. He was a great big lad, whom I had treated since he was a little baby.

Lee had returned for a recheck on his bronchitis. As I was making notes on the chart, I repeated what I was writing: "chest clear, though cough short and harsh persists, especially at night."

"I can make them long and harsh if you really want," he interjected.

* * *

Every youngster, particularly as they approach the teenage years, is very conscious of their physical appearance and most especially of their figure. Every young girl wants to look like Venus, and every young boy would like to appear as Adonis, with the body beautiful. Well, not every child can be so fortunate.

Twelve-year-old Michael was in the office for a general checkup. He had gynecomastia, a not unusual condition that represents an enlargement in the breasts. That enlargement results from extra tissue secondary to the change in hormones the body undergoes during adolescence. His mother asked why he had that.

Before I had the chance to open my mouth, Michael volunteered the cause: "I tried to breastfeed my hamster."

* * *

I must confess that during the holiday season, between Thanksgiving and Christmas, I will sometimes invoke Santa Claus to encourage good behavior. I had just warned Alexandra, who was nearly three years old, that Santa Claus might not give her presents unless she was a good girl and cooperated during the examination.

"I don't want to see Santa Claus," she sniffed indifferently. "I don't want him to come to the house. Anything I want, Big Mom [her grandmother] will get me."

* * *

After finishing replacing his sister's earrings, I waived at her two-year-old brother, Evan. "Bye-bye, Evaroo!" I exclaimed.

Evan looked up at me, bewildered. "Where you going, Doctor Tanis?"

* * *

Ten-year-old Michelle was hiccupping, so her mother told her to hold her breath. The girl immediately grasped her own throat tightly, with both hands, and began squeezing.

*   *   *

Little seven-year-old Theresa was recuperating in the hospital from an infection and the previous day had protested at length that she *really* wanted to go home. Making my hospital rounds, I came into the room and prepared to examine her. Having already looked at her chart and spoken to the nurse, it was clear to me that she was doing exceedingly well. If her examination proved fine, she should be able to be discharged.

Theresa was on her roommate's bed, painting nail polish on the other girl's fingernails.

"Hi, how are you doing?" I asked.

"Fine," she replied, not looking up and still applying the nail polish.

"Um, do you want to go home?"

"No, I really don't," she said nonchalantly, still focused on her work. "I am funning with this girl."

*   *   *

I came into the examining room to see thirteen-year-old James curled up in the seat. "How are you?" I asked, smiling at him.

He yawned. "By now, I'm a little bored. I could have made an atom bomb by the time you got here."

*   *   *

After finishing my examination of little four-and-a-half-year-old Joshua, I gave him a sticker for being a good boy. The sticker had a heart and smiling face on it, with the words "Dr. Tanis loves me."

Following his examination and throat culture, which I had to do because of his red throat, I sent him to the laboratory for a CBC blood test. He left the laboratory in tears and plopped down next to his mother, sister, and grandmother. Suddenly, he ripped off the sticker and wailed, "I don't want Doctor Tanis to love me anymore!"

* * *

It often happened as I entered a room ready to examine a patient that I would be interrupted and called briefly away. As I was preparing to examine four-year-old David, I was given a telephone message that required my immediate attention. Saying to the boy and his mother, "I'll be right back," I stepped away and made two calls.

When I returned, David looked up at me, concern in his eyes. "You go 'potty'?" he asked.

* * *

Three-year-old Jane was in the office because she had been coughing for two months. Because of the harsh sounds in her lungs and the duration of her cough, I ordered a chest x-ray and blood count. When finished, I sat down to write some prescriptions for her.

"You will have to take some medicine," her mother said gently.

"I don't want medicines," Jane snapped.

"Well," I reassured her, "you are so lucky that you don't have to take a shot; medicines are easier."

Jane responded by crawling up on the seat behind her mother and announcing loudly, "I am hiding from my medicines!"

* * *

Little James, a good patient of mine since his birth, was nearly four years old. He came in to see me because his mother had noted some blood in his urine. When I saw him, he had some irritation to his penis and complained of pain in the back and in the flank. I examined him completely. Of course, we got a urine sample and cultured the urine; we did a pinworm test; and we also checked the blood to see the extent of the infection and to assess his kidney function. He went home and was to return with two additional urine samples.

When he came back the next day, the urine culture report was positive for the germ *E. coli*, greater than a hundred-thousand-colony count, which meant that an antibiotic was indicated. I examined him the second day and asked him to lie down, which he didn't want to do. I examined his abdomen and penis. Finally, I said, "Well, you can get up now."

Jumping down, James looked at his mother. "Why does he do these things to me?" he asked plaintively.

* * *

I had finished examining Brent, a six-year-old young man who was a little bit chubby. I touched his chest to pat him. He looked embarrassed.

"I'm trying to skinny up," the boy said apologetically.

* * *

Her examination over, the nurse asked eight-year-old Natalie if she knew where the lab was. "Nat will find it," I said, confidently.

Little Natalie nodded. "I'm an old patient here," she explained, walking past us out of the room.

* * *

Martin, whom I had called Marty-Mart for all of his twelve years of life, was in the office for an examination. His mother asked me, "How long do kids come to a pediatrician's office?" I answered that it was my pleasure and privilege to care for my patients into their middle and sometimes late twenties.

Rolling his eyes, Martin joined the conversation. "Mom," he exclaimed, "as long as you keep on paying, you never overstay your welcome at a doctor's office!"

* * *

Brother and sister, eleven-year-old Kerwin and April, age nine, had chicken pox and were in the office. When I entered the room, April quickly turned her back to me. I couldn't imagine why.

Her mother chuckled and said out of the side of her mouth to me, "April claims that whomever a doctor looks at, he charges."

*   *   *

Ten-year-old Nicole, on her way to camp, had come in for an ear piercing. Her mother mentioned that she was also sporting a bruise on her stomach. After the ear piercing, I asked the young lady to jump back up on the table so that I could look at the bruise.

Nicole, grimacing at her mother, sputtered, "Now he's going to charge me more."

*   *   *

I examined a precious little visitor from Turtle Creek, Pennsylvania, ten-year-old Lindsey. She had an acute inflammation in the outer part of her ear, an external otitis. I asked her, "How does your throat feel?"

She sadly shook her head. "It started to hurt soon's I walked in," she gasped woefully.

*   *   *

David, almost eighteen years old, had come in for a pre-college medical checkup. I entered the room and asked breezily, "How are you?"

He stared incredulously at me for a few seconds and then looked down at himself. "Um, a little bit humbled by my lack of clothing," he replied.

*   *   *

Six-year-old Justin was in the office complaining of pain in the left knee. I examined him thoroughly and failed to discover any abnormality in the motion or muscular strength of the knee. I really wasn't too concerned. His mother cautioned me, stating that he had been more irritable in the last several days. I looked at the chart again and saw that he had lost three pounds in weight. I decided to take an x-ray of the knee and also of the hip, because very often pathology in the hip will refer itself to the knee area—that is, pain will occur in the knee although the trouble is really in the hip.

When the x-rays were available, the mother and I looked at them on my viewing box. "You know," I said, "really and truly I believe that your x-rays are negative. They are normal."

Justin looked up at us, still waiting for an explanation for his hurt. "Then it is growing pains," he finally concluded.

* * *

As I walked into room #2 of my three examining rooms, the mother said to her nine-year-old son, David, "Give Doctor Tanis his poem."

The boy proudly handed me the following poem:

Attention
There are patients in Room 2.
You may have forgotten us, but we didn't forget you.
So, you better get your butt over here or I'll sue.
Because I'm the patient in Room No. 2.

* * *

Seven-year-old Joshua was in the office complaining that his ears hurt. When I examined his ears, both were obscured because of wax. I asked the nurse to flush out his ears.

His seven-year-old cousin, Jonathon, was also present in the examining room. "You're going to flush his ears like a toilet?" he exclaimed.

*   *   *

Six-year-old Katie came in for a visit, complaining of throat pain and abdominal pain. At a previous visit four months ago, she'd had a positive throat culture, which represented streptococcal throat infection along with abdominal pain. Finishing the examination, I reviewed her chart, which showed an elevated cholesterol. "Let's check your cholesterol," I said to her. "It's 247."

Katie looked guilty. "I know, I just ate an egg," she admitted.

*   *   *

Nine-year-old Patrick was in the office because of a sinus congestion. "Do you have a headache?" I asked.

"The only place where I got a headache was in the waiting room," he complained, "where there was all the noise."

*   *   *

James, age four and a half years, was in the office because he would not take eardrops for wax in his ears.

Wagging a finger at him, I said, "You must let your mom give you them."

James slumped his shoulders in resignation. "Well, well, well . . . I just do what you all say," he sighed.

*   *   *

Many of my teenage patients are very private young people. Sixteen-year-old Kevin was in the examining room to have his right groin checked.

"I guess you'll want me to leave the room?" his mother asked.

Before I had a chance to answer, Kevin turned to me and said, "Can you leave, too?"

*   *   *

Elizabeth, nearly eleven years old, was in my office with symptoms of sinus problems—a fever, runny nose, thick discharge, and cough.

"Do you have a headache?" I asked. The girl nodded.

"Where is it?"

"In Connecticut," she exclaimed.

*   *   *

Both Alyssa and Breanna had tinea, a common fungal infection of the skin. "How did they get that?" the mother asked me.

It's often contracted from pets. "Do you have cats or dogs?" I asked.

"Cats," the mother answered. "I guess we'll need to take them to the vet."

Alyssa shook her head. "There goes another two hundred dollars," she said, glaring at me.

*   *   *

I mentioned to seven-year-old Joseph that there was a medication to help his bedwetting, and that it could be given as a nose spray or as a pill.

"I hate nose sprays," Joseph said emphatically.

"When did you ever have a nose spray?" I asked.

"I sprayed perfume in my nose," he replied.

*   *   *

Six-year-old Aida was in my office. I told her to stop sticking her finger in her nose.

"Why?" she asked, clearly puzzled. "My dad does it."

*   *   *

Very bright and competent Hector, ten years of age, was ill with a viral gastroenteritis. He was dizzy and nauseated.

"If you feel the same, I'll see you in the morning," I said. "If you feel better, then just call me."

Looking green, Hector looked down and shook his head. "Actually, it's up to my stomach more than me, Doctor."

*   *   *

I finished a routine complete exam on ten-year-old William—ears, eyes, nose, throat, and all the rest.

"Whew," my little patient said to his mother. "I feel vandalized."

* * *

After I concluded a brief recheck of seven-year-old Alex, he looked up at his mother, bewildered.

"It was that long [a wait] for that short [a visit]," he reflected.

* * *

After finishing examining Nicolos, six years of age, I told him to come back and visit me in one year.

Nicolos shook his head. "I don't know where your house is at," he explained.

Happy Birthday
We ❤️❤️ do
from kids

Tanis
Love you ❤️
John

The Joys of School

Some of my little patients loved school, but many did not. If a medical excuse could be found for them to stay at home, all the better.

Brian, almost nine years old, told me that he absolutely, positively didn't want to go into third grade. "Why is third grade the most important grade?" he demanded.

I gave him all that I had, on the spot: "Because it prepares you for fourth grade."

Brian stopped, thought about it for a moment, and nodded. That settled it, and he was okay.

*   *   *

I announced to nine-year-old Spencer, whom I had diagnosed with pharyngitis (an inflammation of the back of the throat), that there would be no school until his fever was gone, which I expected would happen in twenty-four hours.

Elated at the news, Spencer sprang out of his chair and eagerly exclaimed, "You mean no school all this year?"

*   *   *

One August, I was examining Stephanie. I asked her if she was looking forward to returning to school.

"Doctor Tanis," she announced dramatically, "in three weeks my life is over."

*　*　*

Six-year-old Jasmine was sitting in a tub of warm water because of a urinary tract infection. Out of the blue, she blurted out, "I am in first grade and I have to study and write. I need a day off."

*　*　*

I asked six-year-old Angelo, who attended Boulevard Heights Elementary School, which grade he was in.

"Grade zero," he replied, with a big grin.

*　*　*

Ten-year-old Michelle, the daughter of a representative to the state legislature, had a severe cough. "Will I have to go back to school today after I see Doctor Tanis?" she asked as I was making notes.

"Well, we'll see," her mother said soothingly.

"Of course, school is very important," I interjected. "How are you going to be the first woman president if you don't go to school?"

"I'll get over it when I'm thirty-five!" she declared.

Which is, of course, the minimum age for being president of the United States.

*　*　*

Twelve-year-old Katherine was out of school with a sore throat. During the office visit, her mother asked me, "How tall is she?"

"Sixty and one-half inches," I said. Turning to Katherine, I asked, "How many feet is that?"

Katherine looked at me for a moment, and then turned her head away.

I never give up. "How many inches in a foot?" I inquired.

Looking annoyed, she turned back to me. "I don't know," she confessed. "I haven't been to school for a while."

*   *   *

I asked eleven year-old Giovanni if he was enjoying the summer. He nodded enthusiastically.

"What has been the most outstanding thing that has happened?" I asked.

"The last day of school," he replied earnestly.

*   *   *

Six-year-old Erica was in the office with her younger sibling, Billy. It had been her second day back to school, so I asked what she had learned in school today.

"I learned to shut my big mouth," she sighed, looking embarrassed.

*   *   *

Four-year-old Xavier was in my office when he told me that his big sister was in school. I asked him if she was learning anything.

"Not really," he said gravely. "All she does is draw big circles."

* * *

My patients and I frequently discuss their progress in school. During one such conversation, ten-year-old Brenden wanted to know if it was good to be in the ninetieth percentile.

"Sure it's good," I said encouragingly.

His seven-year-old sister, Brooke, then chose to enter the conversation. "Sure it is," she piped up. Then she paused and added, "You get to have a good view of everyone else."

* * *

Seventeen-year-old Jamie had come in for his second visit during a viral illness that was keeping children home from school. When I asked him how he was, he declared, "Doctor, my white cells are on vacation, and my virus is learning its multiplication tables."

Brothers and Sisters

So many times I saw not just one child but also their sibling. And so many times what they said to or about each other in the examining room was memorable.

Examining nine-year-old Matthew's chest, I heard a few crackles. I asked his mother if he or his four-year-old brother, Mitchell, had been coughing.

"They have both been fighting something," she acknowledged.

"Yeah, fighting each other," Matthew said.

* * *

"Doctor Tanis," Juan began, looking at his seven-year-old twin. "She has been aggravating me since I was four years old."

* * *

I walked in to see my two last patients of the day: Timothy, nine years old, and his five-year-old brother, Andrew. Andrew was covered with paint splotches.

"Andrew, you are the cleanest kid I have seen all week," I said to him solemnly, trying not to laugh.

"No, he isn't!" Timothy protested. "He isn't the most brightest either."

I looked at Timothy and nodded. "How old are you?"

"I am nine," he said proudly, and in the same breath presented his credentials: "I wear a watch."

* * *

Sophia was acting up during her physical examination. Her five-year-old brother, Joseph, shook his head sympathetically.

"This is the worst birthday in her life," he explained to me. She was only two years old.

* * *

Baby Alexander had gained eleven pounds in seven months. I asked what kind of exercise he was getting.

"Eating," his seven-year-old brother informed me.

* * *

Gathering her history, I asked nine-year-old Tynnetta if she could swim.

"Yes!" Tynnetta exclaimed.

"No, she can't!" interrupted her twelve-year-old sister, Travinia.

"I can!" Tynnetta protested.

"She can't!" Travinia retorted, walking up to her sister. "You could drown in a tub."

* * *

Little eight-year-old Patricia and her six-year-old brother, Tommy, were in the office right after Thanksgiving, because their mother had relented on their strict diet and had allowed them to really indulge on Thanksgiving. Each one had experienced some vomiting and abdominal discomfort, but they were a little bit better now. I examined Patricia and sent her to the laboratory to have a blood count taken; then I examined Tommy.

When the lab reports were finished, I sat down and discussed the findings with the children's mother. I decided to tease the little girl a bit. "You know, Patricia," I began, "when you were out of the room, your brother told me that he thought you were the most wonderful girl in the whole world."

Giving me a quizzical look, she pointed to her brother. "I don't think he's normal today," she said.

* * *

When I would come into a room when a young brother and sister were waiting for me, I would often say to the young man, "Is this your wife?" or to the young lady, "Is this your husband?"

This time I asked five-year-old Frank, "Is this your wife?" pointing to his two-and-a-half-year-old sister, Michelle.

Quick as a whip, he answered, "No, she's my daughter!"

* * *

Four-year-old Michael came in complaining of an earache; he also had had a fever the previous evening. While I was examining him, his mother held his little sister.

"Who is that?" I asked him. "Is that your wife?"

"No, that's my sister," he replied. Pausing briefly, he then added, quite seriously, "I've had her for a long time now."

Little Amy was four months old.

* * *

It's routine in pediatricians' offices that the examination of an infant who comes in for a two-week, one-month, and first-year checkup includes measurements of the head and chest. I was measuring six-day-old little Jacqueline, when her big brother, Eddy, who would be six years old the next month, looked at me and nodded thoughtfully.

"I remember when you done that to me," he informed me.

* * *

Two of my favorite patients, Adam, age six and a half, and his sister, five-year-old Mindy, were in the office. Both are somewhat hyperactive, as they are always going . . . and jumping . . . and doing . . . and swinging from trees and walls.

Mindy had a hearing test done and a tympanogram. Suddenly, Mindy came to her mother crying. Her mother thought that she had fallen.

"Why is she crying?" I asked.

"Because she did something I told her not to do," the mother announced, disapproval heavy in her voice.

"God punished her, eh?" I teased.

Without warning, Adam hit her and announced, "God punished her again."

* * *

Six-year-old Lucas and four-year-old Alexis were returning for a recheck on their pneumonia. They were sitting in the examining room with their charming mother as I entered after reviewing their chest x-rays.

Jumping up, Lucas exclaimed, "Do we feel better, our pictures? Do our pictures feel better?"

*   *   *

I was examining three-day-old Malcolm and began turning him over to listen to his back.

"Don't break him," pleaded his three-year-old sister, Bianca.

*   *   *

Mickey, age ten, and his sister Tina, age eight, were deep in discussion when I walked into the examining room.

"Quit talking about a Mohawk haircut," Tina snapped.

"What do you want me to talk about," Mickey retorted, "my sex life?"

*   *   *

I had just finished rechecking Yehudit, an eight-year-old young lady, for her strep throat. After completing the throat culture, listening to her heart, and confirming that her urinalysis was normal, I asked, "Honey, what is your phone number?" We always list a phone number next to the throat culture in case the ten-minute test is negative and the traditional culture shows positive the next morning.

Yehudit had barely finished telling me the number when her three-year-old sister, Sarah, exclaimed, "Wait a minute—that's *my* phone number!"

* * *

Nine-year-old Daniel, always full of mirth, pleasantly accosted me in the waiting room.

"I'm here for two reasons," he said. "For her"—he pointed to his eight-year-old sister, Elisha—"and two, to help you finish your book."

* * *

Jamie, almost ten years old, was in for a recheck examination for streptococcal sore throat. When we had a child with strep, it was our principle to recheck them at the end of ten to fourteen days to be sure that the strep had been eradicated, to verify there was no insidious beginning of rheumatic fever, and to check the urine to make sure that the other potential complication, acute glomerulonephritis (inflammation of the kidney), had not occurred.

I said dramatically to Jamie, "I saved your life from the strep infection."

"Yeah, it could have killed her," her thirteen-year-old sister, Shannon, quickly volunteered, "but would have saved ours!"

* * *

It was the first day of June and children were coming in for their annual checkups. The first to enter was five-year-old Michael and his three-year-old brother, Justin.

Michael proudly showed me his little doctor's bag. I had already outfitted him with a stethoscope, Band-Aids, cotton balls, gauze strips, and tongue depressors. I assumed he had brought the bag in for more of the same today.

As I washed my hands and got ready to examine Justin, Michael put his stethoscope in his ears. As I walked over to the examining table, Michael quickly jumped down from the bench on which he had been sitting and stood in front of his brother.

"Excuse me, Doctor Tanis!" he said, one professional to another.

*   *   *

Seven-year-old Samantha began taking deep breaths for me.

"She breathes well," I said, looking over at her thirteen-year-old brother, Randy.

"That's nothing," he said, rolling his eyes. "I do it for a living."

*   *   *

Eight-year-old Jack was reading a book in the waiting room.

"I want to see that book," his four-year-old sister, Jasmine, said, reaching for it.

"But you can't even read," Jack explained, trying to be patient.

"I can try," Jasmine stubbornly answered, arm still outstretched.

*   *   *

Mrs. T. brought in her three sons, and they were a handful: Innocencio, age eleven; Joshie, eight years old; and Isaac, at the ripe old age of five years.

At one point the mother scolded her middle son. "You are being so mean, Joshie," she said sternly.

"That's his specialty," Innocencio piped up.

*   *   *

Jaclyn had acute otitis externa (an infection of the outer ear canal). As I removed wax from her ear, her eleven-year-old sister, Lauren, held her hand.

Their grandfather smiled at me. "The girls are so close," he said softly.

"Like peanut butter and jelly," Lauren confirmed, not letting go.

Through the Generations

It is very exciting when a pediatrician who has taken care of a moth-er and/or father is asked to see their offspring. I call those second-generation children "the babies of my babies." And don't forget, I have even treated the grandchildren of my patients from long ago. When I retired, at least sixty families boasted three generations of patients who had been seen by me. I won't say the second- and third-generation patients were the most important to me, but they do have a special place in my heart—those families and I have known each other for decades.

A mother was in with her eight-year-old daughter, Ashley, a second-generation patient. "I have a virus," the mother told me, "and Ashley had one."

"A family virus," Ashley added.

*   *   *

Gabrielle was a second-generation patient. "Tell the doctor where you are going for your birthday," her mother urged, trying to make her feel at ease.

"I don't know," the little girl replied, arms folded. "It's all becoming vague."

* * *

I was having a discussion with a second-generation patient, Caitlin, who was eleven years old.

"At home I'm the boss," she remarked, and then added, "for ten seconds."

* * *

Jerry was a former patient of mine. After the physical examination of his daughter, three-year-old Eva, I asked him if he had any questions.

Jerry's face broke into a broad smile. "This is great!" he exclaimed. "Ask the good doctor, just like old times."

He smiled down at his daughter. "It's like going to see the wizard."

* * *

Chris, a two-and-a-half-year-old fellow, came into the office. His mother, Cindy, had been one of my former patients.

She reported to me that her son had looked at her this morning and said, "No school, Mommy! Go to doctor's house. Listen heartbeat. Get sticker!"

Sure enough, he had an ear infection. Besides checking his ears, I did listen to his heartbeat, and the boy did get that much-desired sticker.

* * *

A few years ago my New Year started off with a bang. I was having lunch when the telephone rang—it was a second-generation patient calling me about a third-generation child. The two-year-old boy seemed suddenly to be unsteady of gait and was listing to the right side.

Upset and thinking it was a brain tumor, I apologized to my wife, Maxine, grabbed my medicine bag, and left.

The boy was a rather sweet and cooperative little fellow, allowing me free access to examine him. All was going well until I started my neurological exam and looked into the back of his eyes to see his fundi, expecting fully to see a swollen fundus (the retina reflects a swollen brain with increased pressure).

My examination ended abruptly! A good physician has to utilize all his senses. While I was that close to him, the aroma of alcohol greeted my nose. I had a diagnosis: he was, in a word, *drunk*.

Well, this was New Year's Day. The parents had hosted a party the previous night, and had left half-empty glasses of liquor to be sampled by an adventurous and curious kid.

* * *

I walked into the first examining room in the morning to see little two-year-old David sitting on the bench with his mother awaiting my arrival. David's father had been a patient of mine.

The mother said to David, "What's Doctor Tanis going to do?"

"Doctor Tanis is going to hug me!" the little boy piped up.

The examination experience only got better from there. David cooperated, predicting exactly what I was going to do and when I was going to do it, pulling up his shirt to let me listen to his chest, and turning his head to let me look at his ears.

When I was finished, David looked at his mother and announced, "Doctor Tanis is going to give me a sticker!"

Whereupon, I put a little sticker on his shirt.

What a stark contrast to his father. God love him, he was incorrigible, never ever cooperating on anything. This just shows you that if you wait long enough, good things happen in every family.

Sometimes it just takes awhile.

roses are red
Violets are blue
I am glad your
a Doctor Because
I Love you!!

The Good Doctor

Sometimes the story is about me. Quite often it ends with a good laugh at yours truly.

I helped Kemandre, nearly five years old, down from the examining table. "Thank you, sir," he said to me, sincerely.

That was the first time in forty-two years that a child had thanked me in that way. I have never forgotten it.

*   *   *

A little nine year-old girl patient looked up at me and smiled. "Doctor," she said earnestly, "you're nice. I hope you never die."

*   *   *

Mr. M. congratulated me on my fiftieth year in practice. "Why are you congratulating Doctor Tanis?" his nine-year-old son inquired.

"Because he has been here fifty years," his father replied.

"He'll stay forever, right, Dad?" Morgan quickly asked.

*   *   *

I walked into the examining room to see seven-year-old Arnold. "I'm always not trying to forget you," he said, looking at me seriously.

*   *   *

I was examining a very sweet and observant six-year-old gentleman, whose name was Michael. Studying me for a moment, Michael said, "Doctor Tanis, you have two chins."

Well, a pediatrician cannot allow his patient to outsmart him. I immediately replied, "Well, of course I do. When you get to be as old as Doctor Tanis, you are so smart that there is not enough room in your head for all the brains you have. So therefore the body has provided you with neck space for brains."

"Michael, do you have a grandfather?" I went on, not finished with him quite yet.

"Yes, I do."

"Is he smart?"

"Oh, yes," Michael explained to me, "he is very, very smart."

"When you see him next time," I replied, trying not to laugh, "check his neck and see if he has what Doctor Tanis has."

*   *   *

Very often I had Chinese food brought in for lunch, since I like the highly spiced foods of the Szechwan and Hunan provinces. I usually ate lunch in the consultation room, where sometimes the spicy odors would permeate other rooms. Once, right after lunch, I was discussing laboratory findings with eight-year-old Susie and her mother in the nearby examining room.

"What's that smell?" Susie asked, wrinkling her nose.

"I think it is garlic," her mother told her.

Susie then looked directly at me. "Is it coming from your breath?" she demanded.

*   *   *

I had examined Jamie, a fourteen-year-old young man, who had quite a bit of nasal congestion. He had come in with a fever, a headache, and a cough. During the course of discussing his treatment, he started to blow his nose.

"Jamie, blow one nostril at a time," I instructed him, "so that you don't create pressure against your eardrums."

As I explained, I took out a beautifully colored diagram and showed him a picture of the outer, middle, and inner ear, with specific diagrams of the eardrums.

Looking at it intently, he turned to his mother. "Wow—he's prepared!" he exclaimed.

*   *   *

Unfortunately, if the office is busy, it can take some time for me to see a patient. A nineteen-year-old patient had apparently been waiting for a while and had overheard me going from room to room, chitchatting and bantering with the children and parents. When I walked into the room, she laughed and said, "Doctor, you're such a big kid. I've been listening to you the past half hour!"

*   *   *

I examined Nicole, a precocious three-and-a-half-year-old girl. After reviewing her tympanogram, which was a recheck for an ear infection, I gave her a Buckle Up for Safety sticker. We all began laughing, and I reached over and embraced her mother.

"Why are you hugging my mom instead of me?" Nicole asked, indignantly.

*   *   *

I always like to speak a few words of the language of patients whose primary language is not English. Three new children had been brought to me, accompanied by a delightful mother and father who appeared to be speaking Spanish.

Consequently, I ran through my rehearsed Spanish dialogue as I examined each:

- "Abre la boca" to open the mouth,
- "Saca la lengua" to stick out the tongue,
- "No va a doler" to let them know there would not be any pain involved,
- "Arriba" when I wished them to sit up after examining the abdomen.

Finishing the complete examination and exhausting my entire Spanish vocabulary of perhaps twenty phrases, I smiled at the mother. "You have delightful children but they are very quiet," I remarked. "They haven't said anything to me."

She stared at me, confused. "Oh, that's because they didn't understand you," she began patiently. "You see, we are from Brazil and they only speak Portuguese."

*   *   *

Jarred is the seven-and-a-half-year-old son of our veterinarian's family. His mother had been a former patient of mine, and now it was my pleasure to take care of him and his sister, Jessica Lynn. We were discussing the reason for his being in the office, which was a sore throat. His mother and I then started talking about our pets. She wanted to know how the rash on my Doberman's leg was doing.

Losing patience with us, Jarred interjected, "Is this a veterinarian's clinic or a doctor's?"

The mother was embarrassed by his comment, but I simply chuckled and said to him, with feigned impatience, "Jarred, if your mother and father and sister and I allow you to grow up, what will you be?"

"An insulter," he rejoined, quick as a flash.

Even more mortified, his mother said gently, "That's something you only do with your sister and friends."

Jarred pointed at me. "He's my friend," he said, proudly.

*   *   *

Mr. D. had called about a serious situation. He had been refinishing the floor in the room of his stepson, age twenty, and had found two little pills in a bottle. Very distressed, he had called the office immediately.

When I returned the call, the younger sister, Terry, age five, answered the phone.

"I'd like to talk to Daddy, to Daddy, to Daddy," I said to her. "I'd like to talk to Daddy, would you get him, if you please?"

"Who is this calling?" she asked, properly.

"It's Doctor Tanis."

"Whoopee!" she shouted.

* * *

Daniel, five years old, was a rather pleasant young fellow. One time in the examination room, he turned to his mother and asked, "Mom, when do we go to the real doctor?"

Quite surprised at the remark, she glanced at me and replied, "Doctor Tanis is a real doctor!"

"No, he doesn't hurt," her son explained, nodding sagely.

* * *

Several times I encountered true patient loyalty. Michael, a young patient of mine, had struggled through being overweight and unfair treatment at school. We had shared many things together and have deep affection for each other. Unfortunately, his father's school board insurance no longer was accepted by our office. Until the family could get new insurance coverage with an HMO my office accepted, there would be a delay until I could see him.

His mother called and reported that Michael had told her defiantly, "You know if I get ill I am not going to see another doctor. I have money saved in the bank, so if I get sick I want you to take the money out of my bank account and give it to Doctor Tanis so that I can see him."

* * *

I entered the examining room to take a look at five-year-old Scott; his younger sister, Kimberly, was also there. Sitting in the chair, I began getting information from the mother and writing on the chart.

The little girl suddenly looked up at me. In the same casual way that she would address me as Doctor, or her daddy as Daddy, or girlfriend as Suzie, she said, "Majesty."

After having practiced medicine for decades in Hollywood, I was happy to see that someone finally appreciated my true value.

*   *   *

Sometimes we received compliments from our young patients, and it was always a delight to hear them. Ten-and-a-half-year-old Shane was in for a checkup of his viral pneumonia.

"We can cure it because we have the right medicines," I said confidently.

"And the right doctors," he added cheerfully.

*   *   *

Six-year-old Samantha heard my voice in the hall. "Oh, I hear music in my ears," she whispered to her mother.

*   *   *

Four-year-old Melissa was getting a little doctor's bag for Christmas.

Her mother, very proud, asked, "Melissa, what kind of doctor is Doctor Tanis?"

Melissa looked at me. "*My* doctor!" she exclaimed.

*   *   *

Kendall, age five, answered the phone when I had called to check if she was feeling better. I barely got my name out when she cut me off.

"Don't call here," Kendall told me. "You only want money." She hung up.

* * *

After Christmas, I asked Brendan, nearly five years old, to tell me about his best gift.

"The best gift that I got was . . . YOU," he exclaimed, pointing at me.

Sometimes the comments of patients can make our day, our week, or even our year.

The Poor Parents

In continual orbit around my little patients were one or more parents and sometimes grandparents. Their earnest, sometimes heroic, and often humor-laden efforts to raise the children made for many good stories.

Mrs. S. had brought in one-year-old Michael, an adventurous fellow. "Doctor," she admitted, "he has shown us parts of our home we didn't know existed."

* * *

I asked twelve-year-old Joey, "How is your mom's breathing?"

"She is constipated in her nose and chest," he promptly replied.

"I think he meant I am *congested* in my nose and chest," she said, smiling at me.

* * *

Mrs. P. brought in her daughter, Christina, who was seventeen years old. "With regard to the automobile," the mother explained to me, "she just has trouble with the gas pedal."

Christina rolled her eyes. "But you knew that when I was born," she quickly added.

* * *

I asked Mrs. F. if three-year-old Abraham spoke in three- to four-word sentences. "He speaks in paragraphs," she replied, a bit glumly.

* * *

I advised Alexa, age nine, "Your mom should not need to holler. You should be asking her how you can help her."

"If we did that, we would actually be angels," the girl countered.

* * *

I was discussing extracurricular school activities with seven-year-old Austin when he decided to make a point about his father.

"Ever since I was born, my dad wanted for me to be a Cub Scout," he explained. "Sometimes Daddy makes me *so* proud."

* * *

I finished examining Michael's older brother Darrel, who was fifteen months of age, and then I began to look at Michael.

"It seems he's up all the time and wants to eat," his father complained.

"Well, look," I replied, "he's not interested in girls, he doesn't know about television, so he really has nothing more important to do with his time than eat. What do you want him to do?"

The father looked at me, plaintively. "A little sleep," he murmured.

*   *   *

I went to examine little Mandy, who, despite a history of heart problems and cardiac surgery, was really doing quite well. The nearly one-year-old girl screamed and was very active during the examination. After some time, I turned with some desperation to look at the mother.

"Don't look at me," she said, as exasperated as me. "She's the one who's crying."

*   *   *

Finished examining two-week-old Derek, I concluded that he was really doing very well.

"Well, he grunts and groans during the night," his mother complained.

"Put it in perspective," I advised her. "Isn't it better than if he were howling like a werewolf?"

She just stared at me for a moment. "At three o'clock in the morning there is no perspective," she said flatly.

*   *   *

Rhys, a bright five-year-old little boy, was in the office for a recheck on his ear infection. While looking at his ears, my fingers came upon a lymph gland in the back of his head. It was substantial in size. When I looked at the mother, she said dismissively, "Oh that's an enlarged gonad or something he's had since he was born."

I burst out laughing. "Are you sure you don't mean lymph gland?"

"No," she said, puzzled at my reaction, "that's what they told me years ago."

Well, that became my first ever experience palpating an organ of sexual reproduction in the back of the head instead of down in the groin.

* * *

I was examining three-year-old Andrea, whose grandmother was helping me while her mother held her little brother, Andrew, seven weeks old.

"Ah, what a difference there is between boys and girls," the grandmother confessed. "All Andrew does all day long is eat and scream. I think he hates me, because whenever I hold him he gives me the three P's: he pees, poops, and pukes."

* * *

Waiting for little Vickie's lab work and x-ray, I spied her x-ray lying on the counter at the nursing station. I glanced at it and announced, "Gee, this isn't your lab work."

"Vickie," the mother quickly said, "take it if it's better than yours."

* * *

During my early years in practice in Hollywood, Florida, a drugstore was constructed next to our office. We both moved in at the same time, so Mr. M., the contractor for the drugstore, became close friends with my associate and me. We took care of his children and it was a lovely relationship.

The Poor Parents

One Sunday morning Mr. M. called me to say that his daughter Kelly had cut herself and they'd meet me in the emergency room. I appreciated that as a former corpsman in the navy he was experienced with wounds and had decided it merited my seeing it.

When I saw the cut, I knew that it would have to be sutured, so I asked the father to leave the room.

"Doc," he assured me, "don't you remember I said I was a corpsman?"

"But this is your little girl," I reminded him. "That's different than a patient with whom you have no emotional ties."

"No problem, don't worry about it!" he breezily replied, volunteering to hold her feet.

I started to suture her, singing as I was suturing, and she was a very good little girl. After I had put in the Novocain, a local anesthetic, she gave me no problem. I was about halfway done when the father yelled loudly, "Get a nurse to hold her feet!"

As I turned to reprimand him for raising his voice, I saw that he was turning green and slowly slumping to the floor. I finished suturing while one of the nurses rushed over to take care of him. She managed to revive the father, but he was still on the floor.

When I finished suturing, little Kelly jumped down and went over to him. "Don't worry, Daddy," she said, gently, patting his arm, "you'll be all right."

* * *

Mrs. V. brought in six-month-old Jonathon for an inflammation in the throat. While I prepared to do a throat culture on him, her two daughters kept running around and jumping on her.

I then heard a voice from within the swarm of daughters. "Being a mother is something you can only do at home, Doctor" she said, forlornly.

*   *   *

I was examining Melissa, a precocious four-year-old. Looking over at her mother, who sported a new hairdo, I remarked, "Oh, look, Melissa, your mother has her hair done differently. Doesn't she look lovely?"

"Oh, my sister came over to perm it, the top part. I had the bottom part permed before," the mother replied nonchalantly. "I like it kinky."

After that statement, how could I possibly follow up? The examining room grew silent as I tried very hard not to crack up.

*   *   *

I had finished examining Stevie, two months old, who had had quite a few problems as a newborn infant. His father mentioned to me that his wife thought the baby was a little bit hoarse.

In actuality, Stevie had the usual normal nasal mucous that babies have. I recommended to the father that a vaporizer or humidifier might give some relief, and that he also could use some Ocean nasal mist. Apparently not paying close attention, he immediately protested, "Oh, his grandmother and mother would be really on top of me if I took him to the ocean."

Correcting him, I jokingly added, "Look, I don't mind if you antagonize your wife, but please, never, ever antagonize a grandmother."

He looked at me, wide-eyed. "Absolutely, she is completely out of my league and weight class," he admitted, shuddering.

*   *   *

I've mentioned that waits are common for patients of a pediatrician during crunch times. One time, however, when nine-year-old Kevin appeared in the office, I had only one patient in an examining room.

"Please come on back into an examining room; don't even bother to sit down in the waiting room," I said to the mother, bowing and grandly gesturing for them to follow. "Let me show you the courtesy for something you will probably never experience here again."

"After twenty-five years," she muttered under her breath, "I've earned it."

*   *   *

Returning to the office after a day off, I saw a note on an examining table. It was from the mother of Michael, twenty months old. Scrawled frantically in pencil were the following lines:

"Dr. Tanis!

Help!! He is unbearable and the little one is tolerable, more or less. All in all I am going to end up in a home!!!!"

On the other side of the paper was:

"No appetite

Won't eat

Screams

Won't drink (very little)

What do I do????"

*   *   *

Sixteen-year-old Bibianna came into the office one afternoon with her finger in a splint. It seemed to be more than a jammed finger that we see from basketball, football, and baseball injuries. I explained to her that I wanted to take an x-ray because most likely it was broken.

She was in the examining room with her mother and a gentleman friend. As I was leaving the room, I asked the tall, good-looking fellow, "What do you have that's broke?"

"He broke her heart," Bibianna's mother sighed.

*   *   *

Mrs. C. brought into the examining room two coughing daughters, Jessica, age four and a half, and Amanda, seventeen months old.

"Doctor!" she shouted over the coughing. "Is there a lemon law here? Can I return them?"

*   *   *

As I walked into the examining room, the mother said, "I haven't waited this long since prom."

* * *

The exasperated mother of Andre, nearly sixteen years old, said in resignation, "Well, I can't return you now."

"Lost the receipt?" Andre retorted.

* * *

Mr. S. was more frightened of Nicolas's getting shots than the lad himself. "Hold my hands," he instructed his son.

"Dad, you are squeezing too hard!" protested the four year old.

* * *

Mrs. K. brought in her son, a smallish thirteen-year-old fellow.

"All his friends look like his body guards," she announced. "I heard there's a shot for small guys."

The cure for the greatest killer of children.

...ation Institute of Chicago

City of Chicago

Illinois Department of Tr...

Taking Good Care

Anticipatory guidance is the watchword of pediatrics. When discussing this weighty subject, safety measures such as swimming, bicycle riding, firearms, and strangers are brought to the attention of young patients.

I became actively involved in the American Academy of Pediatrics' "First Ride a Safe Ride," in which we tried to have every infant leaving a newborn nursery ride home safely in an automobile restraint. We also strongly encouraged the use of the child car restraints for children beyond that size. Child patients received stickers printed by the state of Florida that said "Buckle Up for Safety."

Everyone was aware of my abiding commitment to child safety in the automobile—especially the parents. One day Mrs. K. came into the office with her small child.

"Did you put him in his car seat?" I asked first.

"Are you kidding?" she laughed, "I've heard about you!"

*   *   *

I asked five-year-old Joel whether he knew his phone number.

"Sometimes when my mother tells me," he replied earnestly, "it just splits out of my head."

*   *   *

I was discussing bike helmets with Joy, who was ten years old. She offered a unique perspective.

"I don't have a helmet—I need a new one," she declared, firmly, "'cause our heads get bigger when we get smarter."

*   *   *

We discussed with twelve-year-old Matt the need for a helmet for skating.

"We can get a real cool helmet," his father assured him.

"How about an invisible one?" his son retorted.

*   *   *

I asked five-year-old Tyler what to do when he crossed a street.

"Help an old lady," he replied hopefully.

*   *   *

While discussing anticipatory guidance with four-year-old Diamond, her mother asked, "How do you handle street crossings?"

"Go fast so the cars don't get you!" Diamond answered.

*   *   *

Going through the list of anticipatory guidance questions, I asked eleven-year-old James, "Do you have any guns in the house?"

"No, we're heavenly people," he answered, smiling proudly.

*   *   *

Parents as well as pediatricians stress to beware of strangers. I told five-year-old Brooke, "The only people who can pick you up from school are Mommy and Daddy."

"Or Doctor Tanis," the little girl quickly added.

*   *   *

"You know who strangers are?" I asked Anthony, four years old.

Nodding, he leaned toward me. "They have glasses," he whispered.

*   *   *

I asked Isabella, nine years old, if her mother protected her from the sun.

"She puts on five coats of fifty!" she answered cheerfully.

*   *   *

I was discussing pedestrian safety with seven-year-old David. "When you go to school, do you look both ways and hold a big person's hand when you cross the street?" I asked.

"No, we have a car pool!" his five-year-old brother, Doug, informed me.

Growing Up

Every physician's office has among its clientele a group of charac-
ters—none more so than in pediatrics. Children tend to be genuine,
honest, straightforward, and usually sweet. How that innocence
views the years ahead can be moving and sometimes downright
funny. My journeying through the years with them, as they grew
and went off into the world, was so rewarding.

I asked eleven-year-old Ruben a question I like to pose to
all of my little patients: "What would you like to do when you
grow up?"

Without hesitation, he said, "I'd like to go home."

*   *   *

Chase was ten years old and so smart that I saw a bright
future for him. One day I asked him, "Are you going to go into
medicine?"

Looking nervously at me, he whispered, "Do I need it?"

*   *   *

Eight years old, Samantha was poised and very sure of herself. Grinning at her mother, I asked the little girl, "Have you had
any proposals of marriage recently?"

"Not even one date," she sighed, with real regret. "My parents can hold me back on my dates."

*   *   *

Parents inevitably don't want their children to grow up too soon. One time, when I jokingly asked twelve-year-old Rebecca about her marital plans, her father quickly stood up and interjected, "She can't get married from the convent."

*   *   *

Little Ashley was turning ten years old in May. When I congratulated her on the pending milestone, she just shook her head and scowled.

"Doctor, I don't want to be in the double digits," she grumbled.

*   *   *

Brother Daniel added, "I'm four but I will be nine."

Elder sibling Matt, seven years of age, replied, "You don't want to be nine." I asked why.

Matt said, "Because it is harder to be nine; there is more to do."

*   *   *

There always came a point when my office had to say farewell to our little patients who had grown up. The young men and women were not always ready to leave.

I remember one time explaining to nineteen-year-old Shabana, "My associates don't feel comfortable seeing older patients."

"Why?" Shabana asked plaintively. "I can act like a child."

*   *   *

Three-year-old Justin and his mother were in the examining room. As we concluded the visit, Mrs. W. decided to ask her son what he was going to be when he grew up.

Walking over to my chair and hoisting himself on it, the little boy glanced at me and quietly said, "A little doctor."

*   *   *

Tiffany, a precocious five-year-old little girl, is the niece of one of our laboratory technicians. Tiffany was legendary in the office for having choice phrases at her fingertips and putting them to her mouth at a moment's notice.

She had come in this time because of a severe infection. She had a 104-degree fever, and her throat and ears were bright red. I gave her an injection and placed her on medicine.

She returned the next day, much improved, so we had some time for a deep and serious discussion about her future. I suggested that she might want to be a doctor.

"No," she said firmly, shaking her head, "absolutely not."

Her aunt chimed in, saying, "Well, I think that it would be nice."

Tiffany looked at her, incredulously. "No, my mother won't put me through medical school," she explained patiently.

"You know," her aunt continued, not realizing she was out-gunned, "with your mouth it might be better that you be in law school." I agreed with this solution.

Tiffany gave us both a cold, calculated stare. "I think I'd prefer a mouth school," she stated flatly.

*   *   *

I checked the sutured laceration on the back of the hand of fifteen-year-old Brad. The young man eagerly asked if the injury prevented him from working as a busboy.

"That's okay," I said, reassuringly. "Instead of just putting a Band-Aid on it and letting air get at it, as I had thought we might do, we will redress it and you can go ahead and work."

"That's not what I really wanted to hear," he murmured, now deflated and clearly crestfallen.

*   *   *

I walked into one of my examining rooms, where sat seven-year-old Desiree.

"What do you have on your lips?" I asked, peering down at her.

Looking me right in the eye, she said, "Lipstick."

Pretending surprise, shock, and anger, I protested, "How could you have lipstick? Are you eighteen years old?"

"No," she said defiantly, her eyes still locked with mine.

"Well," I sniffed, "you may not wear lipstick until you're eighteen years old."

Desiree narrowed her eyes. "That's *your* problem," she retorted.

*   *   *

I had seen three-year-old Staishia one evening for severe bronchitis. She returned for a recheck.

As soon as she walked in, the little girl proclaimed, "I don't want to get a shot. I don't want to get a shot."

"Well," I replied, "I think I can promise you that you don't have to get a shot."

She then issued a new decree. "I don't want you to put that thing in my throat."

"I think I can promise you that if you open your mouth real big, I won't have to put anything in your throat." I smiled at her. "I just have to look."

With my agreeing to her demands, she was content. I finished her examination and concluded she was recuperating well. As I was making some final notes, I asked my usual question: "Staishia, what do you want to do when you get big?"

She thought hard for a moment, and then a smile lit up her face. "Get a shot," she vowed. "Get a shot on my pinky."

I *really* look forward to reminding her of that in about ten years.

*   *   *

I had just finished examining little Rory, age three and a half years, for her annual checkup. Spying many forms to be filled out on her chart, I turned to her with an innocent expression and asked, "Why do I have to fill out all these forms, Rory? Are you getting married?"

Eyes wide, she stared at me and said nothing.

I couldn't resist. "Are you going to college?"

For the longest time, she looked at me and remained silent. Finally, she sighed. "I'm just growing up," she murmured.

*   *   *

In this increasingly hectic life, pediatricians are confronted by many complaints that turn out to be psychosomatic in origin. I had finished examining fourteen-year-old Lisa, who had come in with the chief complaint of a headache. I explained to her that fortunately we did not find anything bad and that it was definitely not serious.

Her shoulders slumped as she shook her head. "Maybe it's the pressure of life," Lisa said, dejectedly. "I have so much responsibility."

*   *   *

Adam was just a little bit under six years of age and had a father who was a physician practicing pulmonology. They were both in the examining room when I asked Adam what he wanted to be when he grew up.

"A doctor!" he immediately volunteered. He suddenly stopped smiling and abruptly turned to his father. "Dad," he began in a low voice, "what sickness do patients have the least of? That's the kind of doctor I want to be. I don't want to work so hard."

Growing Up

*   *   *

Jorge, a four-and-a-half-year-old young fellow, had just finished his complete examination by me. I remarked to his mother that his hemoglobin was thirteen grams. "He's got the hemoglobin of a teenager," I announced.

"A little teenager," Jorge hastened to add.

The mother laughed. "Jorge doesn't want to grow up," she said, smiling at him.

"Because the girls will kiss me," Jorge replied, folding his arms and looking a bit worried.

*   *   *

Jonathan, a little visitor from Massachusetts, knew exactly what he was going to be when he grew up. "A big bad guy," he told me solemnly.

*   *   *

I asked Danielle, six years old, whether she had a bicycle. "Yes," she confided, "but it shrunk."

*   *   *

After I finished my examination of Liquisha, her mother told her, "Now that you're five, you can help us clean up!"

Liquisha was having none of it. "Not until I'm ten!" she exclaimed.

*   *   *

I was chatting with Robert, age nine, and his mother about school. Was the boy in fourth grade or sixth grade?

Robert declined to answer. "I like it when I'm young," he insisted firmly. "I'd rather be young."

*　*　*

What are you going to be when you grow up? Four-year-old D'Angelo had a surprisingly simple answer.

"Five."

*　*　*

There are certain things that happen in the course of a day in the office that remind the physician that it's all really worthwhile. All the heartache and the aggravation, all the patients and colleagues who are not satisfied, are secondary to an occasional wonderful moment with a patient.

Today a patient of mine, a twenty-three-year-old young lady whom I still see for her annual checkup as well as the occasional illness that she now encounters, came into the office to have a conference with me. I saw her sitting in the waiting room, looking quite solemn.

When I asked why she had come in, she looked intently at me. "I just found out today that I am pregnant."

We discussed the various alternatives. She was finishing college, working at another job, and had her profession picked out for the next year. The young man who was jointly responsible with her would be told that night. She told me that he probably would eventually be her husband, but that neither of them were prepared for a pregnancy at this time.

After a lengthy conversation—for which there was no charge—she made her choice based on her own feelings and reasoning. As she stood up to leave, she embraced me and said, "You are my friend, Doctor Tanis."

The Little Ones
Have Kept Me Young

Practicing Pediatrics

Starting out those many years ago, I and my partner, Dr. Saltzman, worked long hours, including every other night and every other weekend. That included routine house calls, a practice virtually unknown today. Yes, our profession required a great deal of our time, but we immensely enjoyed treating our child patients and getting to know their families.

What was a typical day like in the life of a pediatrician then? I readily admit that I never knew the particular twists and turns I'd be following through any given day of practice, but it always began the same way each morning: my wonderful wife would get up before dawn to make breakfast and pack my bag lunch.

I would first make rounds of the newborn nursery and pediatric ward at Hollywood Memorial Hospital. In the beginning the pediatric ward had six to eight beds separated by glass partitions. Nowadays it boasts two hundred beds for children.

It was fun making hospital rounds, because in the newborn nursery and on the obstetric floor waited the families, whom I taught breastfeeding practices and how to establish a close parental relationship with a child. I had been extremely lucky as a third-year medical student that one of the early pioneers in promoting breastfeeding taught in the pediatrics department.

When he demonstrated the beautiful relationships and healthy babies that resulted from helping new mothers adjust to nursing—nothing comes easy—I was determined to provide breastfeeding education and support for the mothers.

Meeting with parents on the hospital floor, I always stressed that each baby possesses different characteristics—medical, psychological, social—and therefore they should approach and interact with their children as individuals. Each child is a unique person.

Then it was off to the office for the best part of the day—seeing patients. Kids were much more at ease in the office than in the hospital. While interviewing a family and speaking to the child (if they were old enough), I encountered the child's opinions and feelings. So many chats with bright two- and three-year-olds over the years!

I always spoke directly to the children in my office if they were old enough to comprehend what I was saying. Getting their attention, I reasoned, meant that half of my job was done. I invited the parents, usually the mother, to listen in and be part of the conversation, but the kids knew they were the most important person in the room. They were free to come and speak to me directly—and they often did. Sometimes the simple responses were the most telling. When a child made a comment that I thought was unusual, pertinent to the situation, or even important to the extreme, I would interrupt what I was doing. Immediately, before forgetting, I wrote down the remark on a yellow slip from the pad of paper I carried that was normally used for recording my instructions to parents.

My medical relationships were always founded on trust. Parents and patients could satisfy their curiosity by asking me anything. If I didn't know an answer, I stayed with it until I tracked down someone who did.

Sometimes my patients were the children of celebrities and sport athletes visiting Florida, particularly during the winter months. I did enjoy meeting those parents; their children received the same attention and care as everyone else. Many times I later received notes expressing their appreciation for being treated in such a homey fashion.

Our contact with patients was not limited to the office. Those many years ago it seemed that Dr. Saltzman and I made house calls all the time. Despite the hours, I enjoyed seeing the environments in which my patients were being raised; house calls also brought me closer to a patient's family. I will admit, though, to spending extra time with the brand-new parents of a child, trying to anticipate certain problems they might expect, not only to help them but also to minimize the new parents' anxiously awakening me in middle of the night! Some nights my family insisted on coming with me during an evening call to a house. While I worked, they patiently waited in the car, children in pajamas.

It could be tiring, though. Early in my practice, it seemed that for four or five weeks in a row I never got a night's rest, not a single night's rest. The phone would ring, and I would have to get up, get dressed, leave the house, and make a house visit. One night in the middle of a flurry of such house calls, my dear wife and I decided we would stay up late rather than be woken up by the phone. We talked, had a light snack, and then played cards. Finally around 2:30 or 3:00 AM, we both became so exhausted that we put our heads on the pillows and dozed off. Yes, you guessed it—then the phone rang.

As the years went on, the practice of house calls diminished because we could offer more services in the office. Some remembered, though, how we used to do things. One time a Mrs. V. said to my nurse, "I want Doctor Tanis to make a house call."

Shaking her head, my nurse responded, "He doesn't make house calls anymore."

"Sure he does," Mrs. V. insisted, "he called me at home last time," misunderstanding that a telephone call isn't the same as a doctor's traditional "house call."

After an evening house call in the 1950s, I would go to bed. The next day, before sunrise, my wife and I arose and it all began again. At the hospital and office, the children and their parents were waiting, needing to see me, needing to talk. I never stopped reveling in every moment of it.

Farewell

They came to say thank you, to say good-bye. All of them—the little ones, the young parents, the grandparents balancing on a tender knee a baby who had been treated by the same singing doctor who they themselves remembered looking down and smiling at them, long ago.

My father, Dr. Bud Tanis, decided at long last to retire at the age of eighty-one. With the help of my mother, working with Pediatric Associates and Hollywood Memorial Hospital, Dad decided to end on just the perfect note: an epic ice cream party for all the families and generations whom he had treated over five decades.

On Sunday, January 30, 2011, more than two hundred former and current patients and their families gathered in the auditorium of Hollywood Memorial Hospital to pay tribute to their beloved pediatrician. Some flew in from far away; everyone dressed in their Sunday best. Lotsy Dotsy and Strawberry the clowns entertained the children, who, with smiles, brought gifts they had made for their doctor.

Standing at the front of the auditorium, my father greeted and reminisced with everyone, still giving advice when asked. As people waited patiently to speak with him, I walked back and forth in the line, introducing myself and asking how they knew him. Heartwarming and moving stories poured forth, full of deep affection and respect for Dr. Tanis. Before long, I had gained a new perspective on my father, appreciating more than ever before how he had positively affected the lives of so many human beings for over half a century. I was and am so proud of him.

When my father addressed the group as a whole, a baby suddenly started to cry. He simply smiled at the little one, and said, "That's OK, you go ahead and cry."

As the farewell party ended and the hundreds of grateful patients began to trickle out of the auditorium, I realized that they had shown me an important truth. My father wasn't the only one born under a lucky star, I realized. All of us have been equally fortunate and blessed to have had him in our lives.

Elizabeth M. Tanis

Looking Back—
and Forward

It didn't take me long after beginning practice to decide not only to treat children but to become their advocate as well. I represented "my children" throughout Florida and nationally as an officer of the American Academy of Pediatrics. I represented Broward County at the state level and was also sworn in as a lobbyist for the AAP. My committee persuaded the Florida legislature to be the first state to pass a child restraint law (car seats) the first time around, and to require that insurers cover immunizations. The most important function I performed as a doctor was immunizing my patients. I am a strong advocate of vaccines, having seen cases of polio in medical school, diphtheria in hospital clinics, and measles in hundreds of children, including my own. Our Siamese cat Yum-Yum, whom we had for twenty-one years, used to park himself outside the bedroom door of one of my children who was soon to break out with a communicable disease, such as measles, mumps or chicken pox. Yum-Yum always diagnosed it before I did.

Through the years, as our practice grew and grew, I never gave up advocating for children. When I served as the president of the medical staff at Memorial Hospital in Hollywood, Florida, I helped establish the neonatal unit for high-risk babies. Ever a proponent of breastfeeding, I served on the board of trustees for La Leche League International and became president of the International Board of Lactation Consultant Examiners. Looking back, I am very proud of my efforts to support and encourage breastfeeding.

I feel I made a difference—though it all has been a bit humbling at times. I remember being called by several radio stations and one television station to comment after the failure of Amendment 9—a referendum on limiting malpractice awards—to pass the Florida Supreme Court and be put on the November 6 statewide ballot in 1984. As always when making a media appearance, I telephoned my mother and my mother-in-law to let them know.

My wife and I went out to dinner and were joined by some very old and dear friends, who were accompanied by their twenty-one-year-old son, Michael John, a patient of mine for many years. I confessed to them that I was ordering a small dinner because I had seen myself on television, counted my chins, and had decided then and there to go on a diet. I also told them that my mother-in-law had agreed with me that I did need to go on a diet. When I expressed reluctance to call my mother, knowing that she would really tear into me for how I looked on television, Michael John stared at me. "You mean you're still afraid of your mother?" he exclaimed, large eyes open in wonderment.

Why did I eventually retire at the age of eighty-one? I wanted to spend more time with my family and to write about the funny and fascinating things children had said in my office over fifty-four years. At the time I wrote them down, they tickled me and made me smile. Every day listening to children brought me joy and happiness for being a part of their lives, and for getting to know and help guide their families.

I hope that reading this book brings back fond memories of your pediatrician. I am sure that they loved every moment in the office, treating and listening to children, as much as I did. The little ones have kept me young.

ARNOLD L. TANIS, MD, FAAP, is cofounder of Pediatric Associates, first established in Hollywood, Florida, in 1957. He entered the University of Chicago at the age of 14. One of the most prominent pediatricians in the state, he served as president of the Florida Pediatric Society from 1986 to 1989.

CPSIA information can be obtained
at www.ICGtesting.com
Printed in the USA
LVOW05s0824121117
555921LV00006B/31/P